GW01458303

3303711265

BUSTING MYTHS ABOUT

GREAT WHITE SHARKS

BY TAMMY GAGNE

raintree
a Capstone company — publishers for children

Raintree is an imprint of Capstone Global Library Limited, a company incorporated in England and Wales having its registered office at 264 Banbury Road, Oxford, OX2 7DY – Registered company number: 6695582

www.raintree.co.uk
myorders@raintree.co.uk

Edited by Carrie Sheely
Designed by Dina Her
Original illustrations © Capstone Global Library Limited 2022
Picture research by Kelly Garvin
Production by Tori Abraham
Originated by Capstone Global Library Ltd
Printed and bound in India

978 1 3982 2274 8 (hardback)
978 1 3982 2275 5 (paperback)

British Library Cataloguing in Publication Data
A full catalogue record for this book is available from the British Library.

Acknowledgements
We would like to thank the following for permission to reproduce photographs: Alamy/ Nature Picture Library, 23: Getty Images: Boston Globe, 11, JOSEPH PREZIOSO, 8, RODGER BOSCH/Stringer, 28: Newscom: David Jenkins/robertharding, 5, David Middlecamp/TNS, 18, IFA Film/United Archives, 20, Kelvin Aitken/VWPics/ agefotostock, 14, Mark Rightmire/ZUMA Press, 19; Shutterstock: CatwalkPhotos, 29, Charles Lewis, 24, Cq photo juy, 1, Derek Heasley, 10, Kaesler Media, 27, Kris Clifford, 26, MG SG, 7, Rajat Kreation, cover, Ramon Carretero, 13, RugliG, 16, wildestanimal, 6, 17

Every effort has been made to contact copyright holders of material reproduced in this book. Any omissions will be rectified in subsequent printings if notice is given to the publisher.

CONTENTS

Words in **bold** are in the glossary.

CHAPTER 1

A mysterious shark of many myths

The fishermen were almost done for the day when they saw a seal. It was swimming in the open ocean near their boat. The fishermen were not the only ones who had spotted the animal. Just as they were turning in the direction of home, a great white shark broke the surface of the water. It sprang from the water with the seal trapped in its mouth. In just seconds, the powerful **predator** had snatched its **prey**.

The fishermen had heard stories about great white sharks. But they had never seen one so close. They were struck by its incredible size. Great white sharks are the largest hunting fish in the world. Most are between 3.4 and 4.6 metres (11 and 15 feet) long. But some are as long as 6.4 metres (21 feet). The largest great white sharks can weigh up to 2,268 kilograms (5,000 pounds).

Great whites sometimes come up
out of the water as they catch seals
and other prey.

Light and dark

The fishermen had long been told that great white sharks were completely white. But they had seen that this wasn't true. Only its underbelly was white. The rest of the shark's body was slate grey. This colouring allows the shark to blend in with its environment. Seals and other prey often don't see great whites coming before they attack. Sunlight makes the top part of the ocean lighter than the deep part. From below, the shark blends in with the lighter ocean colour. From above, it blends with the darker colour.

A great white shark's white belly and grey back help keep it hidden while hunting.

A great white shark's sharp teeth help it to capture prey.

Perhaps the myth of the all-white shark came from people who had only seen these sharks after they had been caught and brought onto boats. The dead sharks lay belly-up. Anyone seeing them in this position might think that the rest of the animal was also white.

Today, most people know great white sharks aren't all white in colour. But other myths still exist about these incredible animals. They include myths about the sharks' **habitats**, eating behaviours and encounters with people. Let's bust these myths one by one!

FACT

Many people think that when a great white shark loses a tooth, another grows in its place. This is a myth. Great white sharks have multiple rows of teeth that constantly move forward. New rows replace old ones.

A great white shark swims off the coast of Cape Cod, Massachusetts, USA.

CHAPTER 2

Habitat myths busted

Many great white sharks spend time in warm ocean waters. This **species** is often found near the **equator**, where the land and water is the warmest in the world. Ocean temperatures in this area stay around 30 degrees Celsius (86 degrees Fahrenheit). But it is a myth that great white shark habitats are only in the warmest waters. Great white sharks usually live in water between 12 and 24°C (54 and 75°F).

These sharks may travel great distances during their lifetimes. Great whites born in the Gulf of Mexico may travel as far north as Nova Scotia, Canada. Changing seasons can make faraway waters just warm enough. People are seeing a higher number of great whites off the coast of the northeastern United States during summer months. Before winter, they **migrate** south to waters near the Carolinas and Florida.

Smaller sharks cannot create their own body heat. But great white sharks can. The large muscles that run the length of their bodies make this heat. It helps great whites live in cooler waters. In water that is 10°C (50°F), a great white shark's body temperature is between 20 and 25°C (68 and 77°F). The sharks can stay even warmer by swimming near the surface. Water temperatures are warmest at this depth.

The ability to swim in both warm and cool waters gives great whites a wider hunting range than other fish.

Location where Maine's first fatal shark attack happened

Maine's first fatal shark attack

In 2020, a deadly shark attack happened off the coast of Maine, USA. A woman was swimming near Bailey Island when the animal attacked her. A tooth that officials recovered from the attack was sent to a lab. The results showed that it belonged to a great white shark. It was the first recorded fatal great white shark attack in the state's history. Many people who lived in Maine did not know that great whites travelled so far north.

Not always near land

It is also a myth that great white sharks stay close to land. Many of them live just beyond coastal waters. Some even swim into deep areas of the ocean. Great white sharks have been found in water as deep as 1,000 m (3,280 feet).

Some sharks that normally live near California, USA, travel out into the open ocean each year to an area east of Hawaii. Shark scientists call the area the Great White Cafe. Scientists aren't sure why the sharks travel there. Some think they go there in search of food.

How did it become a myth that sharks stay close to land? One of the reasons is probably because most shark sightings happen close to land. People then assume that this is where all great white sharks live.

A great white swims in deep water near Guadalupe Island in Mexico.

A great white feeds on a tuna.

14

CHAPTER 3

Hunting myths busted

Scary films about great white sharks make the most of the myth that these sharks hunt people for food. In many films about great whites, at least one person is attacked and eaten by one of these large creatures. This has led many people to believe that great white sharks feast on people.

Real stories of shark attacks on people may seem like evidence that this is true. Sharks that attack people do bite them after all. But people are not part of the great white shark's diet. Great whites eat smaller fish, including other types of sharks. They also eat seals, sea lions, sea turtles, eels, stingrays and seabirds.

Mistaking people for prey

Why do experts think sharks attack people? Some people say that sharks mistake surfers or other people in the water for prey. The idea is that from below, a person paddling on a surfboard looks like a seal or other type of prey to sharks. Some experts think it's most likely that sharks would make these mistakes in murky waters. Scientists think great whites have excellent eyesight. But they may not be able to rely on it as well in murky waters. This could lead them to become confused.

Usually, great whites ignore surfers. But some experts say the sharks can get confused and mistake surfers for prey.

A great white hunts near southern Australia.

Sharks also might be more likely to attack people when they are excited. For example, a shark may be excited as it is chasing prey into an area. If people are in the same area, a shark could more easily mistake them for prey.

Nick Wapner was attacked by a great white near California, USA, in 2019. He holds his surfboard that the shark bit and damaged.

Curious creatures

Besides making mistakes, what are other reasons great whites bite people? Have you ever watched a baby or toddler put a non-food item in their mouth? They do it because they're curious. Experts think sharks do the same thing! They believe great whites are naturally curious creatures. When they see an unfamiliar object, great whites often want to bite it.

Tasting the object helps them to find out what it is. This may be the reason that some great whites attack people even though they don't want to eat them. Soon after biting people, sharks often let go and don't continue attacking. Unfortunately, the large animals can seriously injure or kill people with just one bite.

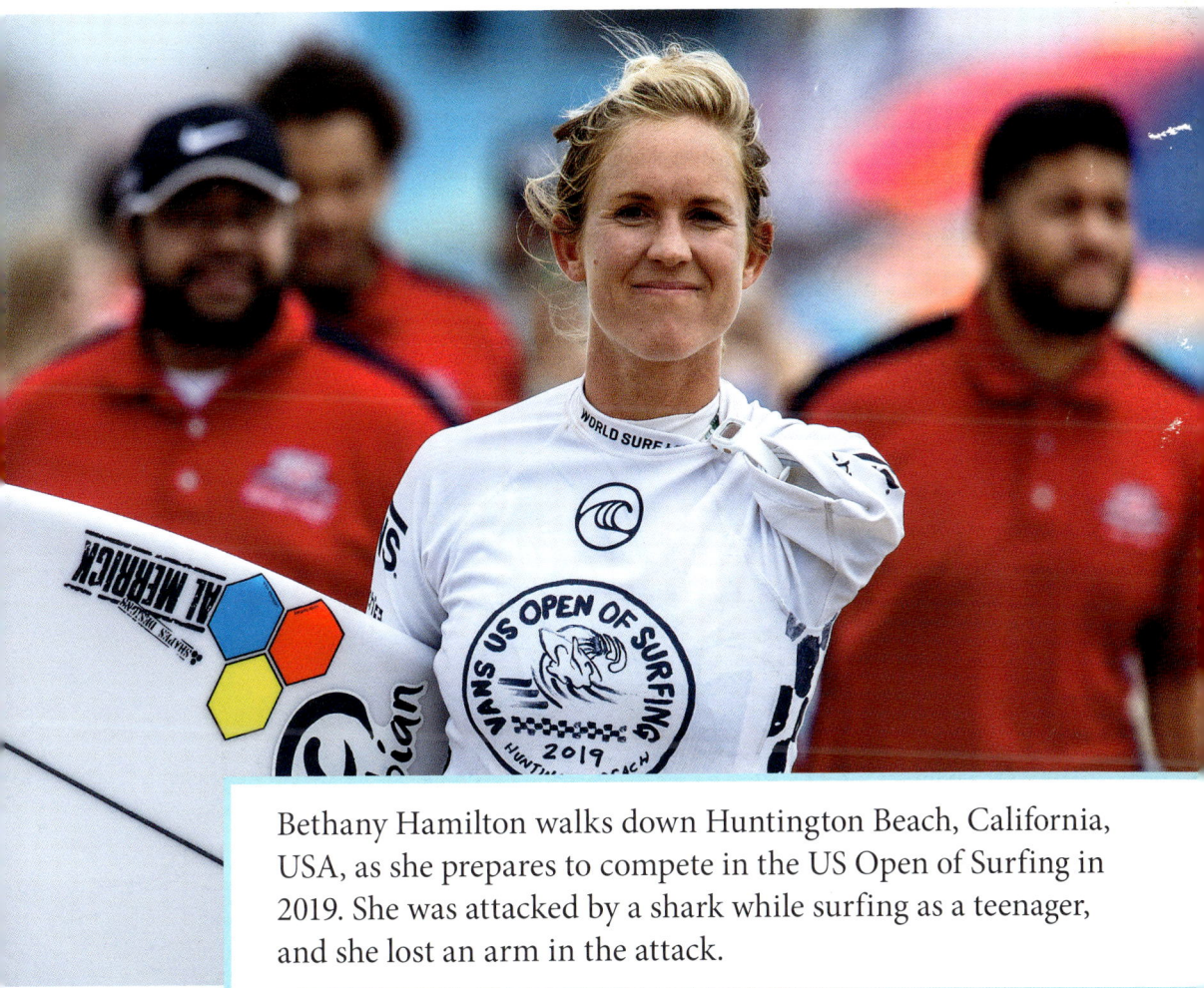

Bethany Hamilton walks down Huntington Beach, California, USA, as she prepares to compete in the US Open of Surfing in 2019. She was attacked by a shark while surfing as a teenager, and she lost an arm in the attack.

In the *Jaws* film, a shark comes up onto a boat to attack people, but this is not natural behaviour for a shark.

Clever swimmers

Yet another myth about great whites is that they have tiny brains and are unintelligent. **Marine biologists** study great whites. They have learned that their brain size compares to that of mammals the same size. They are not mindless hunters who are driven only by an **instinct** to kill and eat. They actually eat very little compared to their body size. They can go weeks without eating at all.

Scary films have also strengthened the myth that sharks target certain humans. These sharks are intelligent, but a great white would never seek out a particular person. And it certainly won't try to get into a boat to attack people.

FACT

It is a myth that a great white can smell a single drop of blood from 1.6 kilometres (1 mile) away. But it can smell a drop of blood in an area of water as large as a small swimming pool.

CHAPTER 4

Scariest myths busted

Great white sharks may seem like frightening creatures. Many people become scared after hearing about an attack. But it is a myth that great whites are a huge threat to people. The truth is that these animals rarely attack humans.

While great whites are one of the most dangerous shark species, attacks on people are still very rare. In 2019, there were 64 unprovoked shark attacks on people worldwide. People cannot find a reasonable cause for unprovoked attacks. Scientists think great white sharks are responsible for about one-third to one-half of these shark attacks. Places where shark attacks occur most often include California, Florida and Hawaii in the United States, South Africa and Australia.

A great white swims near a kayaker off the coast of South Africa.

Cape Cod National Seashore

National Park Service
U.S. Department of the Interior

WARNING

In emergencies
CALL 911

Great white sharks hunt seals in shallow water at this beach.
People have been seriously injured and killed by white sharks along this coastline.

Peak Activity
Based on tagging data

[Sharks may remain year-round]

Know your risk when entering the water.

A sign in Massachusetts, USA, warns swimmers that great whites are often in the area.

Safety steps keep the numbers of attacks low. Beaches may limit swimming to certain depths if a great white has been spotted in the area recently. In some cases, water activities may be shut down entirely for a few days or weeks.

A great white shark attack is a big deal. People bitten by great whites can suffer serious injuries. In some cases, they can lose limbs or even die. But it is also a myth that most great white shark attacks are fatal. The Florida Museum of Natural History tracks shark attacks throughout the world. According to the museum's data, the chances of being killed in a shark attack are one in more than 3.7 million. A person is more likely to die from a lightning strike than from being killed by a shark.

Killing sharks is not the answer

Some people think the best way to protect people from sharks is by killing these animals near coasts. But others say this practice is not very effective. Sharks will continue to have young. They will continue to swim near coasts where people often spend time in the water. Some shark **culling** practices include placing nets near coasts that catch sharks. But sharks can get over and under the nets. Other animals also easily get caught in these nets and die.

By killing too many sharks, prey such as seals could grow in numbers.

PACIFIC OCEAN

■ Sacramento

San Francisco ○
San Jose ○

○ Fresno

CALIFORNIA

Los Angeles
○

N

○ San Diego

■ Red Triangle

FACT

Most great white attacks in the United States happen off the coast of California. An area called the Red Triangle near the northern part of the state has the greatest number of attacks.

Killing sharks is also a danger to the ocean environment. Great white sharks play an important role in the ocean. By eating other sea creatures, the sharks keep the number of those species from becoming too high. If too many sharks are killed, their prey will grow in numbers. These sea creatures will then eat more and more of smaller species. This could lead to many types of ocean animals dying out.

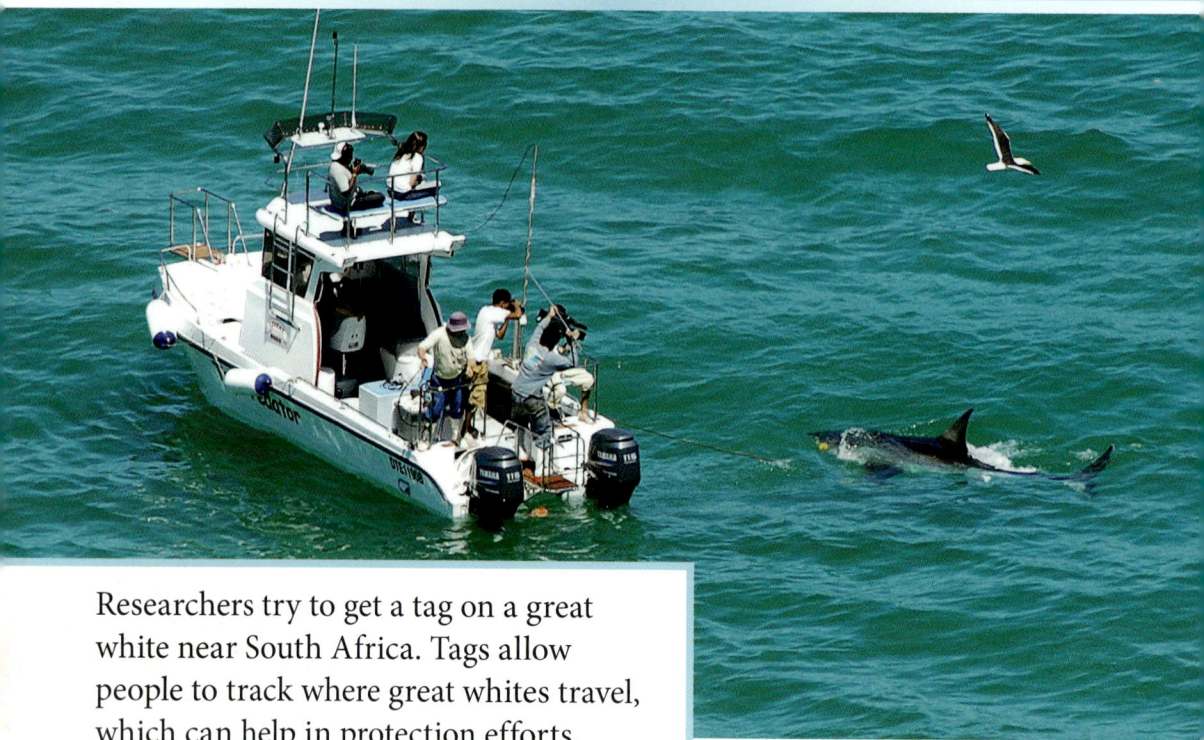

Researchers try to get a tag on a great white near South Africa. Tags allow people to track where great whites travel, which can help in protection efforts.

Protecting great whites

Busting myths about sharks can help people understand the importance of protecting these valuable sea creatures. Sharks help keep the numbers of other ocean animals in balance. Shark **conservation** groups work to protect great whites and other shark species. They help people learn more about sharks. They speak out against overfishing for sharks. Overfishing has caused many shark species to be at risk of dying out.

Sharks have been around for more than 450 million years. By protecting them, we can help make sure that these incredible animals will continue to survive.

Shark fins

The real hunters

Humans pose a bigger threat to great white sharks than the sharks do to us. People kill about 100 million sharks around the world each year. They hunt the animals for their meat. Shark fin soup is popular in some areas of the world. It is also expensive. A single bowl can sell for around £70. People who fish for sharks and sell their fins can make a lot of money. People also use parts of sharks' bodies to make leather and **lubricants**.

Glossary

conservation act of protecting animals, plants and other parts of nature

cull reduce or control the size of an animal population by killing

equator imaginary line around the middle of Earth

habitat natural place and conditions in which an animal or plant lives

instinct behaviour that is natural rather than learned

lubricant substance such as oil or grease that makes a mechanical object's parts move more easily

marine biologist scientist who studies ocean life

migrate travel from one area to another on a regular basis

predator animal that hunts other animals for food

prey animal eaten by another animal for food

species group of plants or animals that share common characteristics

Find out more

Books

Fish (Animal Classification), Angela Royston (Raintree, 2015)

Shark: Killer King of the Ocean (Top of the Food Chain), Angela Royston (Raintree, 2019)

Sharks (DKfindout!), DK (DK Children, 2017)

Terrors from the Deep: True Stories of Surviving Shark Attacks (True Stories of Survival), Nel Yomtov (Raintree, 2015)

Websites

www.bbc.co.uk/cbbc/watch/p00qch9y
Watch this encounter with a great white shark off the coast of South Africa.

www.dkfindout.com/uk/animals-and-nature/fish/sharks
Find out more about sharks and take the Fish: true or false quiz!

Index